THANK YOU,
DAD

WRITTEN BY M.H. CLARK
DESIGNED BY JESSICA PHOENIX

DAD, THIS ISN'T A THANK YOU FOR SOMETHING SIMPLE—FOR ONE MOMENT, OR ONE ACTION, OR ONE THING YOU MADE OR SAID OR DID. IT'S A THANK YOU FOR SO MANY THINGS. IT'S A THANK YOU FOR EVERYTHING YOU HAVE BEEN, AND EVERYTHING YOU CONTINUE TO BE. IT'S A THANK YOU FOR ALL THAT YOU HAVE GIVEN. IT'S A THANK YOU FOR THE PERSON YOU ARE.

BECAUSE YOUR LIFE INFLUENCES MINE. YOUR
EXAMPLE HAS SHAPED MY WORLD. AND THROUGH IT ALL,
YOU HAVE OFFERED COMMITMENT AND SUPPORT, LOVE
AND HUMOR, CONNECTION AND JOY. ALL I CAN SAY IS

THANK YOU,

FOR ALL OF IT. EVERYTHING YOU ARE TO ME
MATTERS MORE THAN YOU KNOW.

WITH LOVE,

_____

...WHAT IS DONE IN
LOVE IS DONE WELL.

Vincent van Gogh

THANK YOU, DAD, FOR YOUR

HARD WORK

✧✧✧✧✧✧ AND YOUR ✧✧✧✧✧✧

BIG HEART.

...THE PRESENT MOMENT IS ALL YOU EVER HAVE.

ECKHART TOLLE

I'M SO GRATEFUL FOR EACH
DAY WE'VE SHARED.

...THE MOST
IMPORTANT
THING WE EVER
GIVE EACH OTHER
IS OUR ATTENTION.

RACHEL NAOMI REMEN

I APPRECIATE THE
TIME YOU MADE.

MAKE VISIBLE WHAT, WITHOUT
YOU, MIGHT PERHAPS NEVER
HAVE BEEN SEEN.

ROBERT BRESSON

THANKS FOR
EVERYTHING
YOU ADD TO
THE WORLD.

YOU'VE TAUGHT ME SO MUCH.

ENCOURAGE ME, AND I
WILL NOT FORGET YOU.

William Arthur Ward

THANK YOU, DAD, FOR BELIEVING IN ME.

...THE LITTLE THINGS ARE INFINITELY THE MOST IMPORTANT.

SIR ARTHUR CONAN DOYLE

I'M SO GRATEFUL

◇◇◇◇◇◇◇ FOR THE ◇◇◇◇◇◇◇

EVERYDAY GIFTS.

LOVE IS AN ACTION,
NEVER SIMPLY A FEELING.

BELL HOOKS

I APPRECIATE
YOUR EXAMPLE.

NO WORK IS INSIGNIFICANT.

MARTIN LUTHER KING JR.

THANKS FOR EVERYTHING YOU'VE GIVEN.

YOUR
GENEROSITY
MAKES THINGS
POSSIBLE.

FORTUNATE ARE THE PEOPLE
WHOSE ROOTS ARE DEEP.

Agnes Meyer

THANK YOU, DAD,
FOR OUR HISTORY.

SOME THINGS DON'T LAST FOREVER, BUT SOME THINGS DO.

SARAH DESSEN

I'M SO GRATEFUL FOR
OUR CONNECTION.

THE MOMENTS OF
HAPPINESS WE ENJOY
TAKE US BY SURPRISE.
IT IS NOT THAT WE
SEIZE THEM, BUT THAT
THEY SEIZE US.

ASHLEY MONTAGU

I APPRECIATE
EACH JOY-FILLED MOMENT.

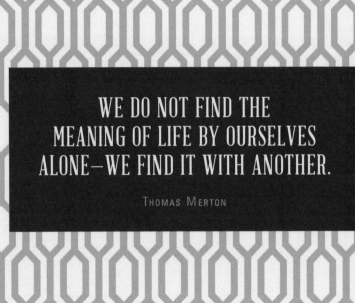

WE DO NOT FIND THE
MEANING OF LIFE BY OURSELVES
ALONE—WE FIND IT WITH ANOTHER.

THOMAS MERTON

THANKS FOR SHOWING ME

WHAT MATTERS MOST.

...HOME ISN'T A PLACE.
IT IS A PERSON.

STEPHANIE PERKINS

THANK YOU, DAD, FOR BEING YOU.

THE MEMORIES I VALUE MOST,
I DON'T EVER SEE THEM FADING.

Kazuo Ishiguro

I'M SO
GRATEFUL
FOR TIMES TO
REMEMBER.

HE WAS BORN WITH A GIFT OF LAUGHTER...

RAFAEL SABATINI

I APPRECIATE YOUR HUMOR.

HERE'S TO ALL THE
PLACES WE WENT. AND
ALL THE PLACES WE'LL GO.

JOHN GREEN

THANK YOU FOR

OUR PAST,

OUR PRESENT,

◇◇◇◇◇◇◇◇ AND ◇◇◇◇◇◇◇◇

OUR FUTURE.

YOUR LIFE
SHAPES MINE.

ONE IS NOT BORN INTO
THE WORLD TO DO EVERYTHING,
BUT TO DO SOMETHING.

HENRY DAVID THOREAU

THANK YOU, DAD,

FOR DOING
SO MUCH.

WE DO NOT BELIEVE
IN OURSELVES UNTIL
SOMEONE REVEALS
THAT DEEP INSIDE US
SOMETHING IS VALUABLE...

E E CUMMINGS

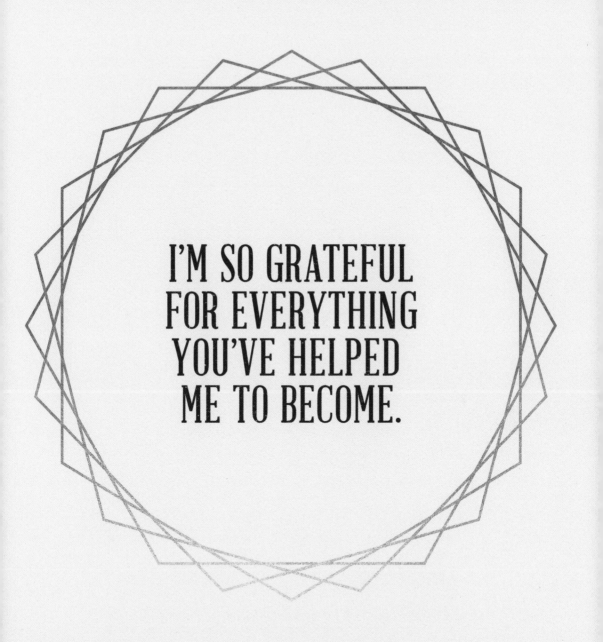

I'M SO GRATEFUL
FOR EVERYTHING
YOU'VE HELPED
ME TO BECOME.

...HOW TRULY
NECESSARY WE ARE
TO EACH OTHER.

MARGARET J. WHEATLEY

I APPRECIATE

WHO WE ARE TOGETHER.

...AS WE LOVE,
WE CHANGE THE WORLD.

Samahria Lyte Kaufman

THANK YOU FOR THE
DIFFERENCE
YOU MAKE.

YOU ARE AN

INSPIRATION
TO ME.

TO DO THE USEFUL THING,
TO SAY THE COURAGEOUS
THING, TO CONTEMPLATE
THE BEAUTIFUL THING:
THAT IS ENOUGH FOR
ONE MAN'S LIFE.

T. S. ELIOT

THANK YOU, DAD, FOR

ALL THAT YOU DO

◇◇◇◇◇◇◇◇◇◇ AND ◇◇◇◇◇◇◇◇◇◇

EVERYTHING YOU ARE.

WITH SPECIAL THANKS TO THE ENTIRE COMPENDIUM FAMILY.

CREDITS:

WRITTEN & COMPILED BY: M.H. CLARK
DESIGNED BY: JESSICA PHOENIX
EDITED BY: AMELIA RIEDLER

ISBN: 978-1-938298-83-7

3RD PRINTING. PRINTED IN CHINA WITH SOY INKS.